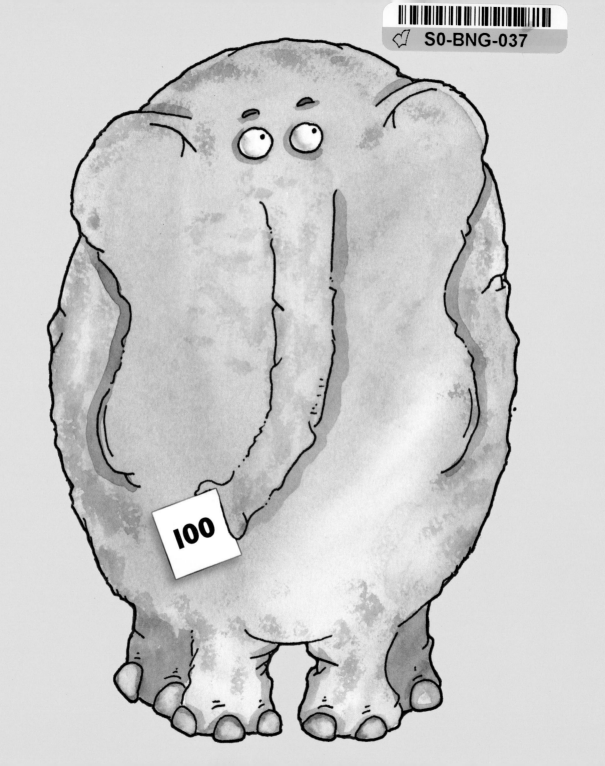

"Be kind to one another, tenderhearted, forgiving one another, as God in Christ forgave you."

Ephesians 4:32 ESV

Kindness Counts!

Written and illustrated by

Debby Anderson

CROSSWAY BOOKS • WHEATON, ILLINOIS

A PUBLISHING MINISTRY OF GOOD NEWS PUBLISHERS

Dear Young Math Genius,
Have fun exploring the 100s chart inside the cover: Point to all the
numbers with a 7. Look for all the 30s. Count by 2s, 5s, 10s. Find the
twins! (11, 22, 33 . . .)!

A special thanks to:
Matios Abebe, Ivan Castro, David Krug,
Caitlin Rasaphangthong, Hayden Williamson,
and to Laura Krug, their photographer.

Kindness Counts!
Text and illustrations copyright © 2007 by Debby Anderson
Published by Crossway Books
         a publishing ministry of Good News Publishers
         1300 Crescent Street, Wheaton, Illinois 60187

Editor: LB Norton. Math Consultant: Kate Bennett.

Scripture references marked NLT are taken from *The Holy Bible, New Living Translation*. Copyright © 1996. Used by permission of Tyndale House Publishers, Inc., Wheaton, IL, 60189. All rights reserved.

Scripture verses marked ESV are taken from *The Holy Bible, English Standard Version*®. Copyright © 2001 by Crossway Bibles, a publishing ministry of Good News Publishers. Used by permission. All rights reserved.

Library of Congress Cataloging-in-Publication Data
Anderson, Debby.
    Kindness Counts! / written and illustrated by Debby Anderson.
      p.cm.
    ISBN-13: 978-1-58134-861-3 (hc)
    ISBN-10: 1-58134-861-4
  1. Kindness—Juvenile literature. 2. Counting—Juvenile literature. I. Title.

    BJ1533.K5A57 2007
    241'.4—dc22   2006032420

L B	17	16	15	14	13	12	11	10	09	08	07
14	13	12	11	10	9	8	7	6	5	4	3	2	1

To Gordon,

The kindest person I know!
I can always count on you!
You are my one and only!

You are

I

in a

1,000,000!

Kindness makes us smile! In the fall, Grandpa helped me plant flower bulbs in a pattern for Grandma. We waited all winter for them to bloom. Now it's spring, and there are 6 flowers! *Acts 14:17*

$$3 + 3 = 6$$

There are 3 red flowers. How many are yellow? How many altogether? What color should bloom next? Which one is the tallest? Which one is the shortest? Which ones are the same height?

bedrooms and sorting everything into buckets.   *1 Thessalonians 1:3*

Which bucket has the most things? Which bucket has the least? Which buckets have the same?

How can I help to sort my sister's teddy bear collection?

I can sort them by size. Which one is the biggest? the smallest? Which are the same size?

We like to sort coins! With our $5, we are buying school supplies for kids who are going through hard times. Kindness means giving and sharing!

Proverbs 14:31

100	pennies	= $1	4	quarters	= $1
20	nickels	= $1	1	dollar bill	= $1
10	dimes	= $1			

100 pennies

1 dollar bill

10 dimes

4 quarters

20 nickels

Kindness helps us to get along together.
Our train carries zillions of zebras and zoo animals!

Ephesians 4:32

ZOO

2 zebras + 2 ostriches = 4 animals

3 penguins + 1 bear = 4 animals

$$4 + 4 + 4 + 4 = 16$$

1 alligator + 3 hippos = 4 animals

Kindness to animals counts, too! *Matthew 6:26*

Which one of Grandpa's bird feeders
   has the most seeds?
Which has the least? Which have the same?

1 dog – how many legs?	5 birds – how many eggs?
4 ears – how many rabbits?	2 cats – how many tails?

Imagine trying
to feed
the elephants!

14

Now the elephants want to play hide-and-seek!
How many elephants hide behind the tree?
How many hide under the umbrella? How many are in the pool? Too
many! How many altogether?

My calendar shows me how many days until my birthday.
I am inviting 5 friends to my party.

Today is June 1. How many more days?
I want to give each friend 2 balloons.
How many balloons do I need?

16

17

What if frogs had birthday parties?

How many balloons do they need?

Sometimes I don't feel like being kind . . . at all!
But I know that God will help me to be kind and forgiving.

Philippians 4:13

There are 2 girls and 3 boys. How many all together?
Who is in line first? Second? Third? Fourth?

$$3 + 2 = 5$$

10
20
30
40
50

God's kindness is like a shower of rain on a hot day!

"So we praise God for the wonderful kindness he has poured out on us . . .

He has showered his kindness on us. . . ." *Ephesians 1:6, 8 (NLT)*

60
70
80
90
100

Count the small raindrops by 10s!
Clue: There are 10 in each row.

His kindness grows in our lives
like cherries on a tree!
It will be fun to share our cherries
with our neighbors!

Galatians 5:22

6 - 2 = 4

Which basket is the heaviest? The lightest? We picked 6 baskets of cherries. Two spilled. Now how many baskets are still full?

Sometimes being kind means getting messy! Mom and I count and measure as we fill jars with Dad's favorite cherry pie filling.

1 + 5 = 6 1 cup of cherries and 5 more cups of cherries make 6 cups of cherries!

Dad and I count and measure boards for a new shelf for Mom!
We use a tape measure and a pencil . . .

4 + 2 = 6 4 inches and 2 inches make 6 inches!

Which collection has the most shells? the least?

. . . But God measures the oceans with His hands.
He weighs the mountains and islands.
He counts big things like clouds and stars.
In His kindness He also counts little things, like our tears
and the hairs on our heads and little lost . . .

Job 38:37; Psalm 56:8; 147:4; Isaiah 40:12, 15; Matthew 10:30

. . . sheep! The Bible tells about a kind shepherd who had exactly 100 sheep. But one day he counted, ". . . 95, 96, 97, 98, 99 . . ." One was lost! So he looked high and low, above and below, up and down and all around . . . until he found . . . the one little lost sheep! **100!** Jesus is our kind Shepherd! Every one of us is important to Him!

Luke 15:1-7; John 10:3, 11, 14

99 + 1 = 100

As you read the story, point (high, low, and so on) with your finger on the page.

If we were to try and count all His kind thoughts about us,
it would be like trying to count the sand at the seashore!

Psalm 139:17, 18

How can we show kindness to others?
Look back through the book and count 2 ways.

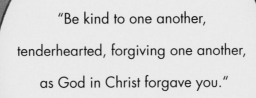

"Be kind to one another,
tenderhearted, forgiving one another,
as God in Christ forgave you."

Ephesians 4:32 ESV

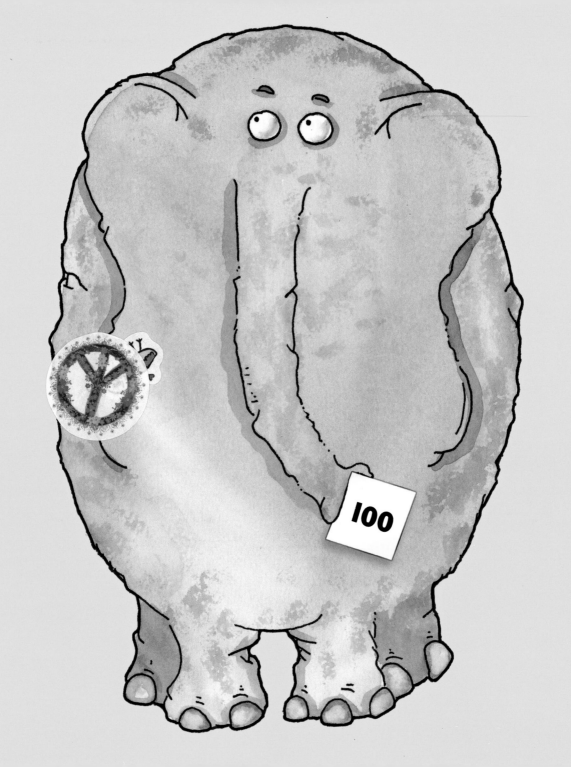